SLA | GUIDELIN

Train to Gain

Continuing Professional Development for School Librarians

Barbara Band

Series Editor: Geoff Dubber

Acknowledgements

Barbara Band and the SLA's Publications Team would like to thank our SLA Board colleague and OSLA chair Jodie Brooks for commenting on the initial draft of this text for us.

Published by

School Library Association
1 Pine Court, Kembrey Park
Swindon
SN2 8AD

Tel: 01793 530166 Fax: 01793 481182
E-mail: info@sla.org.uk
Web: www.sla.org.uk

Registered Charity No: 313660
Charity Registered in Scotland No: SC039453

ISBN: 978-1-911222-09-5

Cover photograph by Richard Leveridge
Printed by Holywell Press, Oxford

Contents

Introduction

Continuing Professional Development (CPD) is not a new idea and many professions require their members to undertake a certain amount per year, either a number of specific hours or by assigning points to various activities. This CPD is often mandated or required by codes of conduct. For example, a nurse has to revalidate with the Nursing and Midwifery Council with at least thirty-five hours of CPD over three years, with twenty of these being participatory learning, in order to continue practising[1] and the Royal College of Veterinary Surgeons recommends one hundred and five CPD hours over a rolling three year period with an average of thirty-five per year.[2]

> *'The RCVS Code of Professional Conduct makes it very clear that veterinary surgeons have a responsibility to ensure that they maintain and develop the knowledge and skills relevant to their professional practice and competence ...'*
>
> —Royal College of Veterinary Surgeons www.rcvs.org.uk

It is easy to see why some specialists such as doctors, architects, lawyers and engineers should maintain their skills and expertise but the argument is not so clear for other specialists, such as librarians. As a profession, there is no statutory obligation to undertake CPD in order to sustain any academic or professional qualifications; although the Chartered Institute of Library and Information Professionals (CILIP) encourages revalidation, this is voluntary and not required to retain a Chartership or Fellowship status.[3] However, CPD is central to demonstrating our professionalism. It is important not only for us personally but also to convince those outside the profession of our value and relevance. We need to demonstrate that CPD is applicable, that it is part of being a professional librarian and that keeping knowledge and skills up-to-date is necessary in order to deliver a high quality service.

This publication reflects on the nature and range of CPD and why it is necessary. It looks at the benefits of CPD – to individuals, our schools and the wider sector; it considers important aspects of efficient CPD and the barriers that prevent us from achieving it; and finally suggests some practical examples of how to undertake CPD in varying circumstances.

---

[1] http://revalidation.nmc.org.uk/what-you-need-to-do/continuing-professional-development/

[2] http://www.rcvs.org.uk/education/lifelong-learning-for-veterinary-surgeons/continuing-professional-development-cpd-for-vets/

[3] http://www.cilip.org.uk/cilip/jobs-careers/professional-registration/revalidation

What do we mean by CPD?

CPD is the concept that we continue learning and developing in our professional roles throughout our working lives. The term is used to describe a variety of learning activities that we engage in to advance and improve our skills, abilities and knowledge. It is not a one-off activity but a continuous and systematic progression of the maintenance and improvement of our capabilities and competencies.

> *CPD is 'the process of tracking and documenting the skills, knowledge and experience that you gain both formally and informally as you work, beyond any initial training. It is a record of what you experience, learn and then apply.'*
>
> —*www.jobs.ac.uk*

The above definition is useful and contains several elements that we need to explore:

Formally and informally – this means that CPD is not just studying for academic qualifications or attending conferences and courses but it also encompasses a whole range of practical skills-based activities and opportunities to engage in informal learning. Thus any activity that helps to develop your skills and knowledge could be considered as CPD.

Beyond initial training – this can be confusing as it is not always clear whether our learning is a part of our job or CPD. For example, reading the School Library Association's *School Librarian* quarterly journal to keep informed about new books could be considered an essential aspect of your role but you are also, at the same time, updating your knowledge. If your school decides to install a structured reading programme, then learning how it works, how to use it and produce reports constitutes new knowledge and could be seen as CPD. We work in an environment that is constantly changing, requiring us to continually update our skills, which makes it difficult to identify when something is a learning activity and when it is routine.

Tracking and documenting – keeping a record of your CPD and its details is essential. This provides useful evidence and gives an overview of your development. I would also add 'evaluation' to this, as assessing the value and impact of your CPD is also important.

It is helpful to have a structured approach to your professional progress as well as developing your work based experience and in this way CPD could also be considered as 'career planning and development.' There are ample opportunities so carefully planning your CPD will enable you to identify that which is more relevant; perhaps engaging in CPD in an area not directly connected to your career position but which links with possible future directions that you might take. For example, your current role may not involve much in the way of web design opportunities or social media usage but you would like to pursue these aspects in future positions. You could complete a MOOC (massive open online course) in these subjects in your own time, learn a range of new skills and perhaps create your own website or blog to use, practise and improve these newly acquired capabilities.

People undertake CPD for many reasons – perhaps for one or several of the following:

- it is mandatory
- to enhance their career progression

- to improve future prospects
- to maintain and enhance knowledge and skills levels
- to demonstrate what they know and have learned
- to validate their professionalism.

CPD is also changing, moving away from formal activities to a more flexible approach that can be adapted to suit one's own circumstances, meaning that you can often access CPD regardless of your physical location, time commitments and financial circumstances. It has become ever more important too. The workplace has changed and we need to be flexible. There are fewer 'careers for life' posts (although I am not sure if this is quite true for school librarians), but we certainly work in a sector that does not remain static; improved and increased use of technology, short term contracts, changing job contracts, the growth in e-resources, curriculum changes, additional teaching responsibilities and shifting teaching styles are just a few of the challenges we face. Most would agree that the role of a school librarian today bears little resemblance to that of twenty years ago. We all need CPD!

Regardless of the reasons for undertaking further training or the methods used, it is important for new professionals as well as those who have been in the sector for many years to ensure their skills and expertise remain relevant, and it needs a pro-active approach; a conscious desire to continue to study, learn and engage with activities, in order to do so.

The benefits of CPD

The skills we require to provide an efficient and effective library service that serves the needs of our school communities will change over the course of our careers. These changes encompass not only library skills but also educational priorities and developments, new ways of learning and teaching as well as changes in technology, and can be triggered by both internal and external factors. This pace of change can be quite fast and is the 'norm' for the world we work in. If you stand still, you are likely to get left behind!

We also work within the education sector where many teachers are keeping their CPD up-to-date. In fact, many schools have an agreed number of statutory INSET days each year in order to facilitate this. However, whilst librarians in some schools attend these training days, what is delivered is often not particularly relevant to them and it would be uneconomic for schools to provide training targeted at only one or two members of staff. It therefore makes sense to seek CPD opportunities outside the school with other librarians. Occasionally this can be done at the same time as teachers' INSET. I have worked for authorities where all local schools have the same INSET days and school librarians have organised training en masse but this is not usual, so CPD often has to take place on other occasions. This can create problems of access and time.

CPD usually brings personal and professional benefits; to us as individuals, to the services we deliver, to our schools and to the wider library profession. These benefits often overlap; for example, a CPD session on the Library Management System (LMS). Whilst we usually only use the basic features of our LMSs on a day-to-day basis and perhaps know little about their advanced functions, time spent looking further at our system should:

- make us more confident with its use
- enable us to produce reports for senior management to show the use and impact of the library
- create a better impression of our capabilities within the school.

Effective CPD demonstrates a strong commitment to self-development, your career, your school and the profession.

The personal benefits of CPD include:

- Increased job satisfaction. Regular engagement with CPD leads to a deeper enjoyment of your work (CPD Research Project 2012[4]). This is a two-way relationship – if you are involved with your job then you will want to learn more and advance your expertise via CPD; undertaking CPD makes you more engaged and committed, and wanting to put ideas into practice.
- Increased confidence and motivation. CPD enables us all to cope with change, giving more control by improving skills and making us more adaptable. This results in less stress and an increase in self-confidence and self-esteem.
- Inspiration and new ideas. People have a tendency to do what they have always done and CPD exposes all of us to new possibilities, concepts and solutions; anyone who has attended conferences or courses can attest to this. You usually finish the day with a list of new ideas you want to implement or at least try out. CPD enables us to keep up-to-date and ensures our qualifications and experience do not become dated.
- Awareness of new or important developments, both within the library and education worlds. This information will enable us to provide a more relevant and effective service.
- Enrichment and development of our role. As solo librarians, many of us work in isolated situations and can become enmeshed with the day-to-day matters and administration of running a busy library. CPD enables us to expand our roles, to set ourselves challenges and to share issues with others in similar positions.
- Career development and enhanced employability. CPD usually helps to identify gaps in our training and gives us opportunities to fill them. It allows us to focus training on specific needs as well as looking at any future directions we may wish to pursue. CPD can also contribute to career progression and achievement of career goals; it informs discussions about work and appraisals, providing evidence of skills. Keeping a CPD portfolio can provide evidence of training to support grade and/or pay increases.
- Demonstration of our professionalism. CPD helps us remain effective and competent, it shows learning agility, exhibits our value and gives stakeholders confidence in our abilities. The capacity to manage CPD is a strength which creates a positive image with employers, increasing our reputation and status.

The organisational benefits of CPD include:

- Better trained and more informed staff. CPD maximises staff potential, ensures skills remain relevant and improves work standards by enabling you to work 'smarter'.

---

[4] www.apm.org.uk

- Added value. CPD brings innovative ideas and practices into the school plus an updated skill set makes staff more productive and proficient.
- Leading by example. School librarians work within a learning culture thus regular undertaking of CPD demonstrates to students and other staff the importance and value of lifelong learning.
- Improved library service and productivity. Increased job satisfaction due to CPD will result in a more committed staff, greater productivity and improved engagement with the service. The reflection, evaluation and assessment of CPD, together with an analysis of its impact, will also enhance its effectiveness.
- Training linked to the school's development plan. CPD helps to focus training and make a meaningful contribution to the school. Effective librarians have an impact on teaching and learning thus CPD will help to indirectly raise student achievement.
- A clear demonstration of professionalism. Schools operate in a competitive market; having a high-quality trained librarian is a 'selling point' that enables the school to maintain an advantage.

It is important to remember that we are all advocates for the profession, that what we do sends a message that can impact and reflect on all of us. Maintaining CPD is good for us as individuals and also for the wider profession. It shows a committed and enthusiastic workforce wanting to learn and to face current challenges and changes. It can also be used as examples of best practice. Academic librarians tend not to have problems with justifying their CPD, (in spite of budget and some staffing difficulties) so why should school librarians have to argue for it? We should be held in the same professional esteem by our employers and in the wider school education world.

The benefits of CPD to the profession include:

- Maintenance and enhancement of professional standards and practice. Individuals undertaking CPD will feed into the body of knowledge for the profession, helping to ensure standards are kept high.
- Advancement of professional knowledge. The showcasing of achievements and sharing of good practice helps to advance the collective body of professional knowledge.
- Professional associations that are able to demonstrate that their members keep skills and knowledge up-to-date. This can be used for advocacy and promotion as well as generating an increase in public confidence in the profession.

Effective CPD

It can be disappointing and frustrating when you attend an event where you feel that the aims and objectives advertised are not covered, even if the training turns out to be useful. We are all busy, we need to be at our desks and therefore have limited training time, so it is essential that all CPD that we undertake is effective for us – it should be of good quality and meet our own needs as well as those of the school – especially if the school is paying for it!

There are some things that can help ensure this: use reputable providers or recognised authorities (and this does not just refer to physically attending courses but also to any reading or MOOCs, etc. that you undertake); ask others for recommendations; and give constructive feedback to suppliers and facilitators so they know what and where they have succeeded or if they have missed targets, and so can try to redress this in the future.

Think about your priorities, both personal and organisational, and try to link all CPD to those defined targets. Be flexible and make your CPD varied, otherwise you will start to find it formulaic and perhaps boring if it is all the same – and you may find yourself lacking in motivation and learning less than you had hoped. Be realistic regarding the amount you can do; it is disheartening to set yourself targets that are unrealistic.

It may be worth creating a CPD audit for yourself:

- Look at what you already know and what you need to learn
- Think about forthcoming library priorities (possibly covering a one to three year period) aligned to the school development plan
- Consider areas/issues on which to focus
- Consider new skills that you feel will really help you to do your job better.

The answers to these questions will help to inform your choices and perhaps your style of CPD – do not forget that you may want to include personal career interests/development too.

The most effective CPD is:

- **Personal** – linked to what you see as your own needs and requirements
- **Relevant** – related to the needs of your library and your school/students and colleagues
- **Sustained** – used and refined over time to embed any new knowledge
- **Collaborative** – many of us work as solo librarians and our circumstances force us to undertake solitary CPD, but collaborative learning can often be more effective
- **Participative** – we all learn by talking and sharing ideas – having conversations (real and online) about what you have learnt and the impact/changes you are making is equally important to reading, listening and note making on our own.

The importance of networking

The last two points are particularly pertinent. One of the most effective and cost efficient ways of engaging with CPD is to exchange information and ideas with other librarians. This is why networking is such a popular and resourceful element of courses and why delegates often say there is not enough time allowed for it during the day. Networking does not have to be in person – it can be carried out just as effectively through online forums on Facebook and LinkedIn or via Twitter Chats and Google Hangouts. In fact, one of the most successful school librarian forums is the School Librarians' Network (SLN), a closed Yahoo chatgroup. To join, send an email to: **sln-subscribe@yahoogroups.com**

It is also often more effective to undertake CPD with others as there is a synergy in the exchange of ideas and information. Remember though; do not restrict yourself to the school library world. Other librarians outside the sector will have similar issues and concerns, and will bring different perspectives. Consider sharing your CPD via articles in professional journals or a blog; writing about your learning, the application of what you have learnt and its impact is also part of the CPD process.

The importance of your CPD portfolio

Create your own CPD portfolio. It does not have to be too complicated or detailed; in fact, the simpler the better as you are more likely to keep it up-to-date. It is easy to create a spreadsheet that records your CPD and has the advantage of keeping all your CPD in one place, providing you with an overview that enables you to track what you do over time. You can also use it for reviews, appraisals, promotions and interviews.

The example below shows you a simple way to record various CPD activities: in addition to the type of activity and hours taken, make a note of why you undertook the CPD and what impact it had (if any) on your work and attitude, and if it resulted in any definite actions. You will note that I add the latest CPD to the top of my list.

Although we all have immediate reactions to the training that we do, it is important to carefully consider/analyse the quality of these activities in some depth – both the good and the disappointing – as this will give you a perspective over time and will indicate what works best for you, enable you to identify the better providers and what CPD and what level of training was most useful.

Questions to consider may comprise:

- what issues were covered?
- what have you learned?
- how you have used this new information or skill set?
- what were the benefits to you and/or your school?
- has the CPD had any influence on your knowledge or the service that you deliver?

You may also want to note comments about the actual training, teaching styles of the provider, usefulness of paperwork given and even if the CPD seemed utterly inadequate for you. This is YOUR evidence so include what is helpful to you. Reflection and evaluation should be a central part of the CPD process.

These sorts of questions and contemplation of the answers will help you to ascertain the usefulness of your CPD and measure its impact. It is easier to evaluate effectively if you have identified a specific area you want to improve, know the tools you will use to measure impact and are given opportunities to implement any new learning. Sometimes the latter is not possible. We often undertake training and then priorities change or we have limited budgets with which to explore new ideas. If this happens, then move on to the next priority or challenge, making a note in your CPD portfolio. Do not make evaluation another 'thing to do' – it should be useful and relevant.

It is easy to lose track of what you have done; the thirty minutes spent reading the SLA's latest issue of *The School Librarian* whilst you have your coffee (or even glass of wine!) gets lost in the rest of the day's tasks, but activities such as these all count as CPD – so take a few minutes at the end of each week to track these achievements. You probably do more than you realise. This is a lot quicker than trying to remember everything at the end of term and you are less likely to forget things. Finally, if you have a LinkedIn profile (or current CV) then keep it up-to-date using your CPD portfolio, you never know who may be looking at it or when that perfect job might come along!

Date	**CPD**	**Comments**	**Time**
18 June	School Libraries Group LibMeet	This is a popular annual event where we discuss current issues in school libraries. It was held in a school library so part of the day included a tour of this – I always like visiting new libraries as it's good to see how others do things – as well as planned discussion through breakout groups. We discussed resource diversity, the suggested CILIP school library kitemark and using picture books. *Result: will be looking at resource provision to ensure the collection is diverse and inclusive. Contact EAL department to get list of students requiring additional support and purchase resources for them. Track borrowing of new resources.*	6.5 hours
8 May	FutureLearn MOOC on Literature and Mental Health: reading articles and watching videos.	The next topic covers depression and bipolar disorder. This is particularly relevant to me as the school library has a pastoral role in supporting students with mental health issues. I currently have several students with stress and depression who work in the library on a regular basis, sent via the pastoral team. I am hoping this topic will enable me to understand the issues they face and support them. We started by exploring the effects of these conditions and how they can impact on daily life. *Result: I created a leaflet on how to deal with stress and disseminated to staff so they can pass on information to appropriate students; I purchased additional resources on stress, mindfulness, etc.; discussed with pastoral team possibility of introducing mindfulness sessions in school. Obtained feedback from staff about use of leaflet.*	2.0 hours
24 April	Reading	Catch up with professional reading including enewsletters from CILIP SIGS and Member Networks, enewsletters from publishers, publications from professional organisations, and educational journals and articles. *Result: Obtained some useful website links to pass on to departments; books added to the wish list. Interested in an article on construction clubs in public libraries – investigated possibility of introducing one of these as an after-school club in library to attract STEM students.*	3.0 hours

Overcoming possible barriers to CPD: taking a positive approach

The usual challenges

Each of us works in different circumstances and we all have varying commitments on our time, money and energy. Both work and life today seem faster paced than just a few years ago and even simple tasks can sometimes occupy a whole afternoon; waiting for a response from somebody before you can proceed with an action, clearing the email inbox, dealing with an unexpected class wanting to exchange their library books when you'd planned to spend the time weeding the biographies. It is easy therefore to let CPD get pushed aside, particularly if you have obligations already in place that make it harder to accomplish anything outside the usual day-to-day tasks. Barriers such as work overload, outside commitments, lack of time, restricted access and lack of funding all militate against doing anything extra, such as CPD.

Too high a workload, too many deadlines to meet and too many obligations usually result in increased stress levels and often the last thing you want to do is add to this with CPD commitments. A work-life balance is also very important. However, do remember that 'time out' for training and networking can actually increase your energy levels and motivation, and keeping your experience and skills up-to-date can reduce workplace stress as you actually feel more confident and in control. Think how it feels when you are using a new piece of software to create resources: if you take the time to learn how it works, you will find it easier to produce satisfactory results; whereas if you try to use it on an ad hoc basis, you are more likely to become frustrated and struggle with it.

Overcoming time constraints

Some people live and breathe libraries! But no matter how much you love your job and would happily spend all hours working on related tasks (and I know several people in this category, myself included) it is important to have some sort of balance with outside interests. Not everyone is in the position to give this sort of commitment, even if they wanted to – many have other demands on their time such as young families or elderly relatives to care for and none of us should feel guilty or pressured into spending our own time on work-related activities. Nevertheless, most CPD will occur outside contracted hours by necessity – so how do you manage to fit it in without signing up to weekends away at conferences or hours spent studying? Time is our most valuable commodity so make your CPD count.

Remember, CPD does not have to be a formal course or qualification; it can be taking part in a Twitter chat for an hour or reading blogs in your break. I am aware that many school librarians rarely manage to take their official breaks but keeping up-to-date is important although why is it that somebody always walks in with an enquiry the minute it looks like you are 'just' reading? Little and often is sometimes the only way we can get it done, fitting in fifteen minutes a day or an hour twice a week. If you commute to work then you can listen to podcasts;[5] if you drive then

[5] https://americanlibrariesmagazine.org/2016/01/04/hearing-voices-librarian-produced-podcasts/

try audio books. We all manage to make time for what we consider is important and this is your job, your career and your future so ensure you give it the highest profile possible given your circumstances.

Overcoming access problems

Some areas of the UK are better covered for CPD opportunities than others, with local SLA branches as well as other groups meeting regularly. However, even if your geographical location means that attending CPD activities is difficult and you have no flexibility to leave the library during the school day, this does not have to be a barrier. There are many online opportunities to undertake CPD regardless of your location, including international activities. If you want to become involved in something more local but it is impossible to meet up, then consider forming an online school librarians group using Google Hangout (for real time communication) or another social media network. This can be a completely private group with limited membership, used for the discussion of specific topics or the exchange of ideas.

Overcoming the challenge of cost

Many schools now run their own INSET sessions for teaching staff in order to cut down on the cost of external providers and most school CPD budgets are likely to be consumed well before they get anywhere near the library! There are ways around this.

- Many schools within the same area have INSET days on the same date so why not arrange for all the school librarians to get together at one school and use the opportunity for effective CPD?
- Look out for events such as LibMeets and Unconferences. These are often run at minimal cost and attendees are usually only charged a nominal amount to cover refreshments.
- MOOCs are free and have the advantage of being able to be worked on in any location and in your own time.
- And let's not forget the numerous blogs, websites, videos, etc. that are available – all free – online.

When you decide to approach your school to request attendance at a CPD activity do:

- Link it to areas of training highlighted in your last appraisal
- Link it to the library's development plan for the current year
- Check your school policy on learning and development as to what it states and do not forget your job description as this may also mention training
- Give senior management all the relevant information – what you will be learning; where it is; the provider; the time and costs involved; and how it will improve your performance and/or your service (the latter is particularly important).

You may still not get permission to attend but giving people as much information as possible will always help your case and show your interest/enthusiasm.

Some ideas and practical suggestions to take you forward

Think positive

Acquiring new skills is an investment. We work in a learning environment; schools and thus libraries are constantly changing and evolving so it is important that we develop and grow alongside them. The issue is often recognising something that may be useful in the future and then thinking laterally about possible CPD opportunities. The following section details a variety of CPD activities with some practical ideas.

Work-based learning outcomes, ie: learning through work experience and practical applications, are as important as formal training and there are many opportunities for school librarians to undertake CPD, regardless of your physical location, constraints or circumstances. As Albert Einstein said:

'Learning is experience. Everything else is just information.'

You can achieve personal development via individual learning in the form of reading, writing, listening, observing, undertaking courses, studying for formal qualifications or through group work such as participating in user groups, networking within your community, representing your school or professional association.

Formal training and workshops: run externally either for a day or weekend

The SLA runs many excellent courses nationwide which are publicised on its website[6] including an annual weekend course, branch and regional courses, an annual member's day and a range of online CPD courses. Members pay a discounted fee.

There are also many courses run by other organisations such as CILIP (via both the School Libraries Group and Youth Libraries Group), the National Literacy Trust, Booktrust and by other independent training providers.

In-house training: for example, INSET days in schools

Whilst much INSET training may not be directly relevant to the school librarian as it is specifically teacher-focused, generic INSET such as safeguarding can be applicable to everyone, so too anything on curriculum development and change.

Studying for a qualification

An academic or vocational course with an award such as an NVQ, degree or post-graduate diploma can be very rewarding. There are several distance learning library-related courses available and if you want to pursue this further, the SLA has links to many of these.[7]

---

[6] http://www.sla.org.uk/training.php

[7] http://www.sla.org.uk/links-training-for-those-working-in-school-libraries.php

Achieving professional qualifications

Such as CILIP Certification or Chartership.[8] There are three levels of professional registration which correlate to your experience and knowledge. The route into all three is the same although they have different assessment criteria. You have to be a member of CILIP to achieve professional registration but there is no requirement for formal academic qualifications.

MOOCs

MOOCs are open access online courses aimed at open participation, delivered via the internet and offer numerous learning opportunities. They usually occur over a period of weeks and are a combination of activities that involve using articles, videos, readings and discussion forums. MOOCs are self-directed so you study at your own pace and in your own time, and their academic level varies. The majority do not lead to a formal qualification but you can pay for a certificate of participation if required. Whilst most of them are not directly relevant to school librarianship, several are indirectly applicable. For example, I have completed a MOOC on 'Education for All: Disability, Diversity and Inclusion' provided by the University of Cape Town via FutureLearn.[9] The schools discussed were all in South Africa, so the children faced very different issues from those in the UK, however some of the concerns and challenges that they faced made me think about the need to provide a more cohesive approach to inclusive education and I could certainly relate several of the matters raised to UK school libraries. FutureLearn was launched by the Open University in 2012 and provides courses from more than twenty UK and international universities and organisations. New courses are being added all the time so it is worth checking regularly. Other useful links include:

- http://librarysciencelist.com/free-online-courses-for-librarians/
- www.coursera.org
- www.edx.org
- www.udacity.com
- www.udemy.com

Reading professional literature

This is an easy way to keep up-to-date in the book, library and education sectors. It can be done at any time via print or online sources, there are several e-newsletters that you can sign up for and getting these delivered into your mail box is a lot easier than remembering to check on different websites regularly. A useful list can be found in the Appendix. There are also many print books on reading, school libraries and education that you can read to increase your knowledge; the wide range of easy-to-read SLA publications are a good place to start.[10] Remember, do not just stick to school libraries but expand your CPD into other sectors as well as education. *Secondary Education* (SecEd) and the *Times Education Supplement* (TES) are often found lying around staff rooms and can provide interesting insights.

---

[8] http://www.cilip.org.uk/cilip/jobs-careers/professional-registration/what-level-right-you

[9] https://www.futurelearn.com/courses

[10] http://www.sla.org.uk/publications

Blogs

Both reading blogs and writing your own. There are many blogs you can follow, written by school librarians, headteachers and other people working in the library or education sectors. There are too many to read them all so be selective; follow those with whom you have an affinity, and enjoy their reading style and point of view. If you find, after a while, that you are not learning anything new or they are not relevant, then unfollow and find some new ones. Try writing your own blog – either as a stand-alone or as a guest on another blog. Talk about your CPD, initiatives you have tried, events you have organised and outcomes achieved. This is a way of sharing good practice as well as advocacy for school libraries and a means of disseminating information. I have my own blog *'Library Stuff'*[11] in which I tend to write about library, reading and literacy related issues. Some others to get you started include:

- www.booktrust.org.uk/news-and-blogs/blogs
- http://teenlibrarian.co.uk/
- https://uklibchat.wordpress.com/
- http://heartoftheschool.edublogs.org/
- http://blogs.ifla.org/school-libraries
- https://community.tes.com
- https://www.theedublogger.com/2015/07/15/23-great-library-blogs/
- http://www.onlinecollege.org/2012/07/10/100-best-blogs-school-librarians/

Other CPD opportunities

- There is a whole range of peer group exchanges available in the form of LibMeets and Unconferences, organised by librarians throughout the UK at minimal cost. Often the agenda and presentations are organised by the attendees so the issues raised will be relevant to current concerns and active involvement allows opportunities to undertake CPD.
- Visiting other libraries – both in schools and other sectors such as public libraries, archives, academic libraries. These often give you new insights into ways of improving your own service.
- Reviewing books for *The School Librarian* and other professional journals and book review websites, including Goodreads.[12]
- Writing articles for professional journals such as the SLA's *The School Librarian*, CILIP SLG's *School Libraries in View, UK Ed Chat* or guest blogs.
- Observation – either watching someone else at work or being watched via reflective supervision or shadowing can be so useful. Shadowing can be difficult for school librarians who are not able to get out of school in term time but it may be worth investigating other schools to see if they have different holiday dates or even arrange this for an INSET day. Observing other librarians can be interesting and often provides

---

[11] http://barbara567band.blogspot.co.uk/

[12] https://www.goodreads.com/

a chance to learn something new. Feedback makes the activity more relevant and useful to both parties.

- Meetings – via local SLA branches and other groups such as CILIP Member Networks, Special Interest Groups (namely the School Libraries Group and Youth Libraries Group – usually open to non-members) and Independent Schools groups. Active involvement in these groups constitutes CPD including attending meetings, delivering training to the group and joining the various committees. You may also want to consider forming your own local school library group to fit in with commitments and geographical locations. The SLA Central and East Berkshire branch was originally a local Berkshire School Libraries group that usefully evolved into a formal SLA branch.
- Volunteering – such as for your local SLA group, governing body or trade union is often an opportunity to learn new skills outside of your current job. This can lead to opportunities for delivering presentations and training, chairing committees and running projects – all good experience for any school librarian.
- Active involvement with e-discussion lists, Twitter and/or Facebook. Many people resist using Twitter but by using it carefully it can be an extremely useful source of information, with links to research, reports, articles, and other CPD opportunities. There can be an element of unpleasantness online but if you are participating in a discussion, for example about books for reluctant readers, then it is unlikely to attract this sort of attention. Official chat sites have moderators and you can control your account and who follows you. I use Twitter to post links to reading and library related events and activities, and retweet similar posts to disseminate information, always keeping tweets professional.[13] Even if you are not active on Twitter but just 'lurk' it can be valuable; there are any number of organisations, publishers and authors you can follow to help you keep up-to-date with library and book related developments.
- TedTalks[14] – TED is a non-profit organisation devoted to spreading ideas in the form of short talks, usually less than eighteen minutes long. The current database, which is searchable by topic, has over two thousand talks and is growing all the time.
- Podcasts – digital audio files – are also another growing medium that you can use to facilitate your CPD. There are many library-related podcasts available online[15] so, again, it will be necessary to be selective.
- Networking with other colleagues, either at formal events or on a more informal basis, which can be either in real life or (as is more the case these days) online.
- Professional discussions with colleagues within your own school. Try to obtain feedback from the staff you work with, your line manager and other colleagues and use this to assess your training requirements. A 'post-mortem' after an event or activity is a useful way to reflect on the process and outcomes.
- Attending exhibitions and product demonstrations such as those for reading programmes or Library Management Systems. Becoming involved in the introduction of

[13] @bcb567

[14] https://www.ted.com/talks

[15] http://www.libraryspot.com/podcast/othercasts.htm

new, upgraded or changed systems and procedures requires training and will increase your skills, so too does taking on additional responsibilities that necessitate learning new or different skills. This may be an extended part of your role but it is still adding to your skill-set and experience.

- Mentoring: this is a really useful two-way process as you learn via the experiences of your mentees who may well have dissimilar ways of working and be in different situations to you. The focus on ensuring that they evaluate their activities will have a knock-on effect on your own evaluation process. Coaching, which is more of a short-term task-based activity, is also a form of CPD, so too the induction of new colleagues including NQTs, new staff (teaching and support) and PGCE students.

Final thoughts

CPD is ever more important to all of us, no matter our library, our job description and role, the school's attitude to the library or our personal circumstances. How we develop professionally and through our schools is ultimately up to us as individuals. Of course make sure that you join the SLA and your School Library Service as first ports of call for advice, help and general support with all things concerning school libraries and school library training. Over and beyond that there are just so many varied opportunities to discuss, study, attend, join, network, read, write and generally enjoy CPD in the 21st century that simply every school librarian can find a useful way to take part, feel good and develop skills, knowledge and confidence in their role, maintain a CPD portfolio and use that training and knowledge to become more effective in what is one of the best jobs in any school. Good luck with your CPD!

Appendix: E-newsletters

- *The Bookseller*: news from the world of publishing – www.thebookseller.com
- Booktrust: research, reports, resources – www.booktrust.org.uk
- Creative: aimed at those working in the creative industries but is useful if you are interested in web design, if you undertake any creative work in the library, etc. as has some great ideas that you can use/adapt – www.creative.com
- Disability in Kidlit: articles, reviews, discussions – http://disabilityinkidlit.com
- Down The Rabbit Hole: http://tinyletter.com/dtrhradio
- Government Email Alerts for Education, Training and Skills: www.gov.uk/education
- Gurteen Knowledge: a global learning community with a focus on knowledge management, learning, creativity, innovation and personal development – www.gurteen.com
- NATE: National Association for the Teaching of English – https://www.nate.org.uk/mailing-list/
- National Literacy Trust: monthly e-newsletter detailing recent research, reports and initiatives – www.literacytrust.org.uk
- Peters Books & Furniture: http://peters-books.co.uk/news/
- Publishers: many publishers produce regular newsletters. Whilst these are mainly for marketing purposes, they can be a useful means of keeping up-to-date with what is being published.
- School Library Association: if you are a member, make sure you have signed up for the monthly e-newsletter – www.sla.org.uk
- Teen Librarian Monthly: http://teenlibrarian.co.uk/category/teen-librarian-monthly/
- TES Weekly Register: https://www.tes.com/news/school-news
- UK EdChat: online magazine, resources – http://ukedchat.com/